poems

Eleanor Goodman

NINE DRAGON ISLAND

HK Enclave Publishing House

飞地书局

Printed in Shenzhen, P.R.C.

Acknowledgments:

"Mahjong," The *Anthill* (Sept. 2015); "Affair" (portfolio of finalists for the Drunken Boat Poetry Book Award), and "Piety (IV)," *Drunken* Boat 21 (Spring 2015); "Boy," "How Cancer is a Reminder of Other Pain," "Les Restes," "Wanting Out," "To an Old Farmer," "In Praise of Dumplings," "Weekend Getaway," "For Once," "Allowance," *Enclave* issue 6 (2013); "Discipline," *Cha: An Asian Literary Journal* issue 21 (Dec. 2013); "On the Plane Back to Shanghai, I Contemplate My Father," "Obey, Obey," *Turtle Island Quarterly, issue* 1 (June 2013); "Operation Enduring Freedom," Oma's Testament," "On Vacation in Vermont, My Father Foresees His Death," "Mangosteen," "Dressing," *Poetry East-West,* issue 6 (Summer 2013); "Ancestry," "To Leave Zimbabwe," *Mantis* no. 11 (Spring 2013); "Near Heidelberg," "Night, Plowing," "Swimming Lessons" *Terrain.org* issue 30 (Fall 2012); "Night Train," "Alleyways, Shanghai" *Cha: An Asian Literary Journal* (Sept. 2012); "By the Sea in Rain," "Iceland From the Air," "Alpenglow," *Sugar Mule* no. 41 (Aug. 2012); "Sanctum," *Cha* issue 14 (July, 2011), nominated for a Pushcart Prize; "Man in an alley off Jiangsu Lu, Shanghai," "Discipline," Charles River Journal issue 3 (Summer 2010); "Piety (II)," *The Best American Poetry website* (July, 2009); "Return," "Fault Line," *Poetry for the Wenchuan Earthquake: A Poetry Anthology,* Nie Zhenzhao, ed., Shanghai: Shanghai Foreign Languages Education Press, 2008; "Hummingbird," *New Delta Review* vol. 14 (2008); "Piety," *Eden Waters Press* vol. 1 (2008); "Ohio," *The Pedestal Magazine* no. 42 (2007); "To an Old Farmer," *Wilderness House Literary Review* no. 12 (2007)

Zephyr Press acknowledges with gratitude the financial support of
the Massachusetts Cultural Council.

massculturalcouncil.org

Zephyr Press, a non-profit arts and education 501(c)(3) organization,
publishes literary titles that foster a deeper understanding of cultures
and languages. Zephyr books are distributed to the trade in the U.S.
and Canada by Consortium Book Sales and Distribution [www.cbsd.com].

Cataloguing-in-publication data is available from the Library of Congress.

ZEPHYR PRESS
www.zephyrpress.org

For my father

CONTENTS

1   For Once

4   Ancestry

6   Les Restes

7   Outside Muncie, Indiana

9   Sustenance

11   To an old farmer

13   Harvest

15   On Vacation in Vermont, My Father Foresees His Death

17   Oma's Testament

19   Dressing

21   On the Slope of the False Peak, My Father Looks for His Grave

23   Ohio

26   Obey, Obey

28   Wanting Out

30   On the Plane Back to Shanghai, I Contemplate My Father

31   Since the Divorce My Mother Never

33   Allowance

38   How Cancer Is a Reminder of Other Pain

40   Piety

44 Swimming Lesson

46 Hummingbird

47 Weekend Getaway

50 Sanctum

52 By the Sea in Rain

54 Operation Enduring Freedom

55 Boy

56 To leave Zimbabwe

58 Fiel

60 Alpenglow

62 Iceland from the Air

63 Near Heidelberg

65 Dance

67 Night, Plowing

69 Foreign Tongues

71 Gift

72 Piety

76 Nine Dragon Island

82 Affair

83 Night Train

85 Man in an alley off Jiangsu Lu, Shanghai

86 Mahjong

88 Mangosteen

89 Six-Foot Chopsticks

91 Fire Conforms to What It Shapes

93 Fault Line

94 Return

96 Beggars Outside the Chengdu Train Station at Noon

98 Hope

99 In Praise of Dumplings

101 On the Second Day of Her Trip to Beijing, My Mother Loses a Tooth

103 Discipline

105 Then, Something

For Once

Mind's mute talk rings louder than twigs snapped clean,
       the self that schemes to pick itself apart.
  Too soon these slopes will cast the shades of fire
        then overnight blow bare and show their bones.
Like city stains flushed from the flesh of lungs,
       each smudge asserts a claim of memory,
flesh ever ephemeral. Leaves loosen
    more vermillion further north, more fallen.
               To lose all but the bones, to be stripped down.
Pale birches blush in the cooling late light,
    evergreen needles slough off to the stream
        where rounded rocks reveal their ancient course.
                    Suffering,
              silence, broken—
        I break too,
a clatter-hoofed deer bolts from the clearing,
    her fear-lashed blazing gaze shock-constricts me—
she dashes, catches her legs on brush, tail
    whipping white—
              call to love, call to danger.

Here the mountains look like mountains the ocean looks like ocean the city gleams like dragonscales
the ocean looks like ocean the city gleams like dragonscales there are trees here that grow on no other island and
fruit that tastes of salt there are trees here that grow on
no other island and fruit that tastes of salt behind the fruit market is another fruit market
where prices are never written down signs behind signs where alleys entwine with traversals

the center shifts around its other center Reclamation Streets light fixture and sealvin stores
Cantofop, men cutting steel by the park in baptismal showers of sparks

Ancestry

My father
whose first memory is flying

from his mother's hands
out the second story window

caught by a neighbor
below on the Niederstrasse

taught me to pick
up pennies for luck—

at seventy he still bends
on bad knees for coins.

Oma leapt after
from that burning house

to escape Berlin
and the bombfire

sprayed by the country they fled to
through slogs of hunger

and the unwelcoming Alps—
for years she kept boiled eggs

and a stub of sausage
in the pocket of her rose-scented apron

so the children wouldn't
go hungry again. Four wars later

none of which I've seen
I winch out nickels wedged

between bricks in Harvard Square
and the homeless men with wired bodies

under layers of sweatshirts in August
watch me in my silk scarf and heels

and once one asked me
where the hell

I'm coming from

Les Restes

My mother's voice drifts down the hallway.
She's talking to herself again,
sorting through the old papers
one page at a time. This afternoon
in the garden of her father's house,
she will be thinking of the work that must be done,
the clearing of rooms, emptying of closets and cupboards,
decisions of what to give away and what to discard—

and I will be thinking of her
and of the cleaning I will someday do
of her things, the remnants of her life,
these objects unconvincing in the absence
of their owner.

Yes, to look at things and see them as they are,
not as we would have them be.

The sound of my mother, finally,
calling from her room down the hallway,
saying it is time for us to go now, it is time
to put on our shoes and raincoats.

Outside Muncie, Indiana

the Air Force sells itself with billboards—
a female fighter pilot, FREEDOM
emblazoned by her head,
stars and stripes serving
as backdrop. Mile after mile of bean rows
and the collapsed

silos of farms
parceled for flat tract housing.
The neon gas station serves
hotdogs to truckers, farmboys
lost to the trades. Inside town limits,
liquor stores

and dueling bondsmen—
Bad Boys Bond Posting and Reliable Bonds,
like parents disagreed over strategy.
A pandaria for the new Latinos
the Army hopes to move out.
This itch to desert

what we've known,
the barrenness of home,

earth resisting all
but violence to bear more fruit
each fall, a blankness that looks lush
from a distance.

After sundown,
Gaslight City is soot-coated
and along unlit rural roads
the lines dead-end into lawns.
On the Indiana Interstate,
the minivans

        crawl along, miles
of shuddering tankers
run diesel down to Kentucky
to the warble of rural radio,
and the teens rev their frustrations
into the dark,

safe, safe—
but feeling like nowhere.

Sustenance

As shadows crept cross furrows,
we gouged the ungraded soil
hunched over the rows like gleaners.
Evening stretched low,

the mild sun dropping
like dandelion seed
without a breeze to buoy it.
Laura comes to watch,

our medicated neighbor,
pretty, broken, not without charm—
she offers a wheelbarrow
of dirt from her yard.

Fertilizer and loam turned into beds,
up to our boot-tops in clay,
not enough worms for the work
no spade or rake can do.

The season of growing
stumbles in, surprises us
like a guest risen too early.
We are loath to waste

this temporary warmth,
to let the lettuce lie dormant,
the pea tendrils' fingers
wilting before pods are born.

Does she look lonely to you,
you suddenly ask me.
What the earth bears, the labor
of hands, desire's distilled gaze—

is there forgiveness to be found
in the loss of self in other,
in the need of an old lover?
I wonder if you might

not still love her.
Under the Seed Moon
we sow each other's lies,
risking the touch of late frost.

To an old farmer

Under the cover of late
autumn dusk I walked

into your fields
and broke the stems

of six yellow apples
off a single bough.

I tried to leave all
the leaves. But so much

has already fallen,
too many of your apples

are lying to rot back
to the roots, half-eaten

by animals that know
safety only in darkness.

I saw the light on
in the kitchen

and wondered
if you sat watching

through the night-opaque pane
or were already asleep.

Each day a bit of strength
seeps away, back to the roots.

I stole your apples,
six sweet from the tree.

Forgive me – I knew
then as I know now

the fruit is not ours to reap.

Harvest

The man at the end
of the street sold his unruly emus,
the neighborhood's most exotic collection,
and asked a friend, a farmer
with his own sixty acres,
to help with the autumn's apple harvest.

He won't run the cider press –
they'll feed the pigs what the market won't take.
Next fall, the fruit will rot back to earth,
the barn in disrepair.

Corn grows yellow in unopened husks.
Late summer roses still unpetal on the front steps.

Down the road, a stranger pounds
nails into the skeleton of a house.
The new foundation strains against the stay of the earth.
But the slats won't last as long as the tree would have
        lived,
if given the chance.

The nature of this world –

does it frighten or comfort him now –
the home not yet standing will fall.

On Vacation in Vermont, My Father Foresees His Death

He brings me a will scribbled on yellow legal paper.
Blood prophesy runs in the family—
in glooms of tea leaves
he sees himself swerve,
a child or an animal
in the road.

on the way to Karme Choling

A lone crow calling
after dark when daybirds
have no business being awake,
the graveyard on the hillside
overgrown.

Protective by instinct, by duty,
tonight fear radiates from his body
and infects the air.
He wants to go inside to the light.

don't let your sister take the house

The moon is an unmoored eye.

crow   *crow*   *crow*

It comes at night,
with snores of shredded charcoal
from his room,
steady, stopping, steady again

Oma's Testament

When I gave up my eyes,
I learned vision is a passage
of billowed silkscreens
covering the thousand doors to truth.

When I gave up my friends to the war,
I saw we never loved
ourselves enough, fearing
the judgments of strangers.

When I gave up two tongues
to a new country,
I wondered what man
had ever been convinced by my words.

When I gave up my children
because it hurt them
to see me, I knew
they had grown strong without me.

When I gave up the need to eat,
I was glad.

When my bones loosened,
I could not see, could not speak,
there was no one. So this life asks nothing
of the dead, and the dead ask nothing of it.

Dressing

Years after the burden
of two babies

my mother gives her nakedness
as a gift—

a porcelain statuette,
not statuesque, but

matronly, a Mayan
idol—her single breast is a white teardrop

on her belly. Flesh-shadows
and faded hair, spidered stretchmarks

she blames on me,
jokingly. To have this figure

after all she's been through
is no disgrace, someone might say,

and she does. Even a daughter is an intruder.
Her body like her love

too easily overwhelms us.
I watch her

appraise me—
we have the same bones—

a warning of what will come
from puttering

in an empty house, nowhere to go
and no way to fight

the body's slow disintegration.
The old desire

to disagree is gone.
Now what is left—her, this

flesh, my hands
helping her into her slip.

On the Slope of the False Peak, My Father Looks for His Grave

He scrapes lichen
from headstone carvings,

uncovering names.
We've climbed all morning

and the path outlasts us—
we make peace with a rock

overlooking a two-eyed lake
that stares up like a mute calf.

He doesn't say
what he's found.

Summer cottages, trout
buried under whitecaps.

My father calls
in his keening voice

to the mountain gods
who have led him here.

Moose tracks, indigestible bone,
two crows shriek back in unison.

The sun ducks its head
behind ash trees,

the air beginning to sting.
We make the world

with the seed of our thought.
Unwelcome words

wither in my mouth.
Heading down, my hand

harnesses his shirt like a child's.
His balance wavers, legs

soft as slow-rotting pines,
and then arm in arm

we steady together
and go on.

Ohio

I never said goodbye to you, Frank,
to listen one last time
to your self-apologies and broad Cleveland accent,
or to hear a final roar
from the sports car you bought
when your girlfriend took her children back to Coshocton,
or to hear your casual atonal strumming,
or smell the odor of canned salmon
coming from your kitchen late at night.

Or to you, Dick, the guy downstairs
whose ex-wife drove to fury
night after night, and whose weekend daughter's
softball team gave conniptions. Dick,
whose banging was always
a mystery, coming up through the pipes
every morning at four. Who carefully
closed my car door to the street
the day I packed up my things.

And goodbye to you too, garden,
our deliberate jungle,
you flourishing bug-haven, tempter

of rabbits, attractor of neighborhood envy.
Your lushness was our pride, waiting
to wither come autumn. Oh pepper
plants, oh tomatoes—I wanted you
before you were ripe, before the earth
was ready to give you up. Goodbye

bike path, swallower of hours.
Goodbye corner coffee shop
and your angst-ridden denizens.
Goodbye grand old houses turned into condos,
and river whose brown touch
I coveted despite all the warnings,
whose rebuilt banks drew box turtles
and buzzards and the occasional hawk.

How many hours did I spend at your curves,
hoping to catch at one of your weirs a heron
or liquidy carp, tadpoles of tree frogs,
goldfinches, bluebirds, a snake on a rock?
So long bread-oven, producer of three loaves
a week, and the faceless coworkers,
those valiant eaters of sweets.

Goodbye to the humid, neck-burning heat.

And goodbye to the farm of four generations,
the silence of cornfields
so supreme that to speak
was some kind of sacrilege.
Goodbye, goodbye bean fields with leaves
as soft as an old woman's cheek,
goodbye llamas, you delicate creatures
of whim and alfalfa. Farewell Richwood,
town of land barons and land
soon to be barren.

Goodbye riches of love, your alluvial ground—
to love is to make a wish of loss.
Goodbye to the farmer's wife self,
the baker, the selfless half-lover,
the grower of herbs.
And goodbye, sweet big-handed one,
whose life had no need of art.

Goodbye to the girl who thought life was over and it was.

Obey, Obey

Your mother made the earth obey her will.
Not like your father did—no chemicals,
no machinery, no engineered seed.
Her hands were her tools, wrinkled and twisted
from hauling boys around by their collars,
cutting fat into biscuits with her fingers.
At the height of summer, she stood sweating
in the kitchen canning collards, Kentucky
wonders, summer pickles, jellies of gooseberries,
chokecherries, grapes from your Aunt Helen's vines.

Her garden was a jungle of lust,
thrumming with honeybees and horned worms, aphids
she plucked off and crushed without anger.
She mothered her boys the same way—the time
your brother crashed his motorbike back the lane
and ran home without half the skin on his face.
Or Jim, who caught his hand in the combine
and lost a forefinger. The granddaughter
born too soon with translucent skin,
so delicate the sun feared to touch her
until she was back in the earth, and Grandma
Dora who drove her wagon into the fence
and had to be watched every minute.

Once we seeded squash together with beans,
row after row in the heady heat,
and she stopped mid-dig to meet my eye.
We'll make a farm wife out of you yet. She meant
my hands would learn the silken slip of loam,
would learn to pull up thistles by the roots—
she meant my hands would come to look like hers.
She could see I was spreading
out from under the shadow you cast.

Tonight in the Indian summer evening,
after a dinner of store-bought sweet corn,
I crave the feel of earth on my skin.
I am putting my hands into tiny pots
by porch light, potting soil and cuttings,
a Swedish ivy that may yet propagate,
as hardy as a city plant can be,
and I smell drifting up from the street a hint
of fecundity, someone's autumn-rotted
morning glories, an uprooted shrub,
a row of caved-in carved pumpkins on a stoop.
In the plickplock splash of rain on the pavement
I hear her words again.

Wanting Out

When Lorraine loses her hair
and the energy to love,
her husband leaves her for someone
who doesn't cough up blood in the night.
He leaves behind the kids and a few old friends,
their new evasive gazes.
She is a wave reflecting off a swimming pool's edge.

And all the wasted worry of last year's
trip to the beach, her thighs fat wedges
in a bathing suit, the kids' misbehavior
and the sting of sunburn spreading
across her freckled shoulders. And on the phone
with her sister, no confession of fear,
of bone fragility and the bruises.

Hospital trays and permanent lights like a prison cell
while outside a night guard chuckles
at a sitcom and eats grapes.
The children visit. Life continues.
We disturb it and add tubes. Friends say hope
is an unpredictable elixir—
they offer ginseng, Essiac, God, Brazilian herbs.

But Lorraine says no
to mechanized breath, no
to priests and specialists, to catheters, to drugs,
no to someone else's blood.
She says no to life without life.
Now what's left is the letting go
of what we think she should have said.

On the Plane Back to Shanghai, I Contemplate My Father

Crows hovered by the road
to the airport, full of hunger—
the frozen lake is a silvered moccasin,

the river phosphorescent on its descent
to the sea, crisscrossing a riven country.
Ohio's red-tipped trees

line the hedgerows,
their red buds dying in ice,
crystal-preserved.

The silver wing descends
through darkened cumulous
and disappears into the smog below.

Stark mirroring—
someday our flesh
will dissolve into oceans.

Since the Divorce My Mother Never

Since the divorce my mother never
    speaks
        his name aloud.

                Your father
she says which is to say
        something happened
            without

permission,
        without her knowing
    until it was in motion.

Twenty years later she calls me
        from Texas
    where she's wed a librarian

        to say in a small voice
Sometimes I wonder
    if the divorce
    made you afraid
            of marriage.
            And I say
            Of course it did.

I say it to hurt her
    and she knows it
        but it works.

            But what I mean to say is
    I am afraid
and
    it wasn't your fault.
   It wasn't your fault or my father's fault.
    It wasn't my fault
  or my hapless
      brother's fault
    or the fault of the relatives who
      never liked her
        or the fault of those who never liked
him.
It wasn't the neighbors' fault or the cat's fault
          or even the fault of an
affair.
   It's nobody's fault. No one's at fault.
        And for god's sake
    that's something
   to be afraid of.

Allowance

Chamomile tea cools in the coffee decanter.
Enrique worries, says Oma refuses to drink—
plump, legs weakened by sugar in the blood,
the stairs insurmountable.
Always keep an egg in the house so the children won't starve.
The summer in the desert she sent me in search
of tortillas still shaped by women's hands,
meine kleine Engel, she called me
eyes already blind to my failures.

                    *

Estranged daughter, a granddaughter
obsessed with making amends—
these paltry comforts. In the kitchen,

Oma's blindness is an oak
spreading its roots beneath the house,
breaking stone, stealing water.

She's been awake for hours, waiting.
Four countries, nine tongues, and the stove forbidden,
the kettle, the fireplace forbidden.

*

After the vision of her death, the months of suffering ahead,
she came out on the porch to listen to my father pull away,
leaning hard against the railing, head cocked like a robin.
his first visit in five years, his last. Distance, shame, a hole
in the sleeve of her sweater. Still hurt by outward things.
Winter, one hand cradled the hollow where her womb once was.

*

The dining table laden with equatorial artifacts,
unopened envelopes, Japanese prints,
yellowed animal bones carved into boxes.
Mixed loyalties.
Stay, have something. There's plenty, bitte, bitte.
Loneliness. She strokes her fingers
down the stained napkin.
These habits that own us.
She is looking into nothing.

*

Enrique, the family mystery, the fake cousin
half her age. He loved her first in the heat
of the Yucatan, now cares for her in our absence.

Felixe, he says. *Felixe.*
Don't forget how hunger feels, Szuzhika. It always returns.
How can I throw a stone?

Sit, break bread, savor—togetherness
a complex need. This tangled triad of women,
my organs torn. My aunt wants to leave her.

*

We found half a photograph hidden in her dresser—
she is fit at forty, round-bellied, bent over her flowers.
She cried the summer the drought came

and she had to let her desert garden die.
A man's torso bows to the cilantro.
We take guesses at the excised face.

Separate realm, plains of wild maize and buckwheat.
You are calling, calling.
The prairie winds lift and carry you.

        *

Shadow-haunted as a child, my aunt bears death
encapsulated in the axis of her spine. Woman
whose bones are kindness, whose love I discover
has its limits. Compassion fails her in this divided house.
Whose love can encompass every fault?
Her eyes will not meet mine.

        *

She accepts our weaknesses
as fitting, as her due.
Oma, regret is my demon,

the same harrowed spirit who raped you
in the sage-haze of your death trance.
Oma, your body was the least of you.

I listen, lips sewn shut
with ribbon. I watch you chew each raisin,
each ruby of sweetness,

savoring, savoring, savoring.

How Cancer Is a Reminder of Other Pain

After her coma my mother
lost her molars.

Oncological nurses
couldn't care less about teeth, she said,

and I wasn't there. Soft gaping gums
and a wound for a breast.

When I was twelve
she stayed in bed for days,

in mourning for her marriage.
I brought her trays

of bouillon and crackers
she didn't eat.

We tried to understand
with the small brutality of children—

studying her dissolution
like homework.

We left each day feigning normalcy
and each night crept past her room,

fearing the oppression of her voice,
while our father counted us

among the casualties.
We cannot save each other.

Now I look for lost things
never finding what is mine,

what is not.

Piety

We do not bury our dead—
they stay or leave as they please.
Burnt sage and rosewater,
in cantilevered dreams

Oma's ghost comes calling.
These are debts
no one knows how to pay,
a magical lineage

the cynical dilute.
For years she roamed
the fields of buffalo grass alone,
seeking some kind of solace.

The Yucatan owls
perch by the window,
their little beaks like scythes.
Offer oranges on the altar,

offer sage and cinnamon.
Now nothing escapes her,
nothing pleases.

She rouses the others

as the living are closing their eyes.
We ask what she wants,
and she speaks with streaks of ash.
She wants us to come with her.

Here the mountains look like mountains the ocean looks like ocean the city gleams like dragonscales
the ocean looks like ocean the city gleams like dragonscales there are trees here that grow on no other island and
fruit that tastes of salt there are trees here that grow on
no other island and fruit that tastes of salt behind the fruit market is another fruit market
where prices are never written down signs behind signs where alleys entwine with traversals

the center shifts around its other center Reclamation Streets light fixture and sequin stores
Contofoot, men cutting steel by the park in baptismal showers of sparks

Swimming Lesson

On top of your body
propped on rocks
by the shale promontory
and shadow of the lighthouse
with its implications
too obvious to limn
where foam gathered
and broke in the kelp
with spits and sprays
the sea growing ever
more greedy and these
are still your environs
despite the estrangement
your dark eyes darkened
by my questions closed
with the divided heat
of your body beneath me
I looked out to where
there was no land beyond
to that imagined harbor
and the island of thirst-
easing olives and fish-skinned
fruits you promise

without meaning
to show me and thought
of what it would take
to make it
how far out I could swim
on my own
if I leapt

Hummingbird

When I injure you, as I must someday do,
my silence will be like a poison drained
from a wound, and like a hummingbird,

a desperate hour short of starvation,
whose wings are incapable of rest
though small, I will dart away

so you may heal from my absence.
And in your blame, which is right, which
is fitting, think back to the first spark

of encounter, the moment you sensed
with our still-palpable animal sense
that I have always been poised for flight

and to clip these wings is to kill
the iridescent body they keep aloft,
and the heart, frailest of birds,

despite love, despite all, still longs to beat.

Weekend Getaway

Saturday morning was too cold for a walk,
finally something to agree on.
On the promontory's rocks where tidal miasma
coats the flaking shale in salt, the air shocked us—
the icicles clenched in the fissures between crags,
forcing them apart. I crawled across the berm
like an over-armored crab and the thin
salt air stung the scrapes on my hands.
From your perch on a dark curve of bedrock,
you stared at a trawler pinned on the horizon.
Gulls gathered over the swells culling fish
and I knew why the ocean is a body,
as raw and saline as we are, death at each boundary.

Roadside shacks, signs for gasoline
and blueberries, muddy and stippled by snow.
I wanted to stop to watch Penobscot's stunted forests
splintering the ocean into green needles,
but you said it should be better further on.
The water was arranged with stark white tarpaulins—
anchored schooners of the rich, covered
against winter squalls. A gray municipal park,
granite dedication to the war dead.

I snapped photographs as mallards
scavenged fish from each other's mouths.
In a motel off Rt. 1, a pastel expanse
of bed, screaming Raptors from the base.

Your mouth in the unnatural dawn
defined what couldn't be salvaged—
a minefield of silences, the smell of slow mildew
staining our jeans—no question of turning around.
Gas station coffee and another rural highway.
We left the car by a meadow of stubble
to search for signs of the St. Croix.
Sandy grit clung to the road's shoulders,
shrinking from our boots. Near the black-edged
clapboard church, a summer cottager's lawn.
You, always more timid, hung back,
while I hopped the fence, hearing the grass snap
like the sound of locusts in a field.

I followed lines of frost across uncertain solidity
and in the shallows by the cove's leeward edge,
two men were bending over the tide flats
to pull clams or whelk from the narrow eelgrass.

Water came up to the brims of their waders

and only the seagulls spoke as they dropped their catch

into a bucket—bivalve, slow-moving, mute.

We know no other way of being.

I heard you approaching, but my only muscle

is the simple lever to open and close me,

and I couldn't swim away, out to where land

dead-ends in bright exposure—

beyond the sullen salt marsh, hoary and bristling, the
    ocean.

Sanctum

for Da Lizi

In the age of hunger
your grandparents' hut
clung to the curve of the river
where it wound round empty rice paddies
and gurgled song

irretrievability   replicas

white-rimmed blue of a schoolboy's uniform
supplicants at the gates of *Zijincheng*
the chaos of fecundity like Jiangnan fields before the
        famine
like cities packed to bursting

lit joss in the temples
prayers for sons and prayers for rain
dragon eyes bought and sold in the market for flesh
burials by the riverbank, your maiden aunt's grave

the girl your uncle bought, her folded hands
the thin soil that bore no more than clumps
water-laden mules, your father's starved mind
after captivity levied by spite

these lives measured and doled out in rations

Damaged love
I will be your absent mother, your uncles, the early-lost
    sisters
the country you left on your way to me

By the Sea in Rain

The rain-laden gales

that force the gulls, fighting, seaward,
and tip us like buoys, lift
the scarf's fringe above my head, Salome tossing

her veils seeking violence,

blow a kittiwake chick
off-course—
flimsy, flapping with conscious or is it

instinctual fear, knowing

only the gilded swoop
back to land,
that current slipping

like an eddy against the rush—

struggling, belly to the whitecaps,
he seeks equilibrium and then
tasting the safety of the shore, yaws

and sails himself

further out to sea.

Operation Enduring Freedom

Sun screams out like insults
in an unknown tongue. Where sand denies shelter
their legs and arms lie crossed, hands mimicking prayer

or thrown across half-closed eyes like children dropping
into sleep, plagued by heat. Flak jackets and khaki boots,
any clarity camouflaged to sand's shade.

No color. No shade.

A helmet has rolled away, an empty husk. The city contracts
like a viper before it lunges,
gathering venom in the pockets of its neck.

Rustling from the red horizon, a stray scuttles past.
They endure, these separated four.
The emptiness around them yawns

and lets them in.

Boy

They have the white sheet
stretched on the ground for him
before they lay the body across.
Too much, too much!
this faded pale boy. His ribs
are dark shadows down his chest,
each bone figured in his jaw, temples,
his tiny wrinkled feet.
The hands that cradle him now
must feel as though they are empty.

This one will rest, and more will come
to feed the earth with the rich
dark marrow of their bones.
They are the bitter progeny
of a barren landscape,
nurtured by the thin milk of the hills
until there is nothing left.

The dregs we drink with our wine;
the gristle of meat we spit on our plates.

To leave Zimbabwe

you must cross
the gray corpse

of the Limpopo River
balancing your life

on your head while
crocodiles

with dried mud eyes
skulk the bank

when you crawl
on your belly

from the dank muck
of the war

they come for you
their teeth

rip you open
and the wound

will fester and swell
into a burden

carried on your back
like wet kindling

Fiel

Not long after you leave
this town and its freezing river
you will drive out
to the northern beach in winter
where the wind will take
your breath and break it
on the cliffs
and you will discover
an opalescent conch
at your feet by chance
and bring it to your ear
and with its salt exhalations
it will whisper to you: where
is Manuel, poor girl,
where is your mouth?

And you will hate him
with the ferocity of the faithful
and the wind
pregnant with meaning
will touch your cheeks
like a white-gloved hand
like a painter's perfect eye

or whistle through your teeth
through the back of your skull
and you will want nothing else
but to be alone with the sea,
to be exposed.

Alpenglow

A river cuts its own path.
It has never needed us,
never needed more than snow
reaching its infinitesimal limits,
running in rivulets
to meet the river halfway.
Everything joins,
the valley and cliff's talus,
the footprints of shepherds
so old they appear
as fossils in the moss.

We live in enormity
in praise of the salamander
and the tadpole, busy at their work,
in the sun's growing shadow
across the eastern peaks.
In praise for the woodsmoke
and the woodsman chopping
in the rain. And praise the rain
bringing life to the forest
year after year, and praise it
in those years it doesn't come.

Praise the forest, all its denizens –
the singers and leapers, the red-
roofed huts, those preyed upon
and those trailing the shivers
of underbrush. Praise the brush, praise
the fearlessness of waterfalls
through the fall of evergreen,
praise the growing and immovable,
praise the incomprehensible,
the ancient, the overtaken,
the Alps.

Iceland from the Air

There can be no there there
vastness more vast
than ocean
part ocean the sudden
volcanic plateaus
the snow peaks nothing
like whitecaps this
land as solid
as forest but a hint
of green nowhere
the fields of cultivation
of man's struggle
to meld world to desire
houses sprout like mold
and how when
rain brings wet scree
in summer and in winter
only snow to stifle
the mountains to
cover the un-fields
of this unremediated light

Near Heidelberg

                    a broken queue of students
claiming love, the quay
of tethered boats
and in the pines
beyond the burg

the river like milk
through moss-covered cliffs.
Unbearable thingness
of things—an extinction of frogs,
a betrayal of need.

Memory in stones and
the lace of too-white edelweiss
in mourning, our mistrust
a waterfall
stricken by weirs.

This immobilized tributary,
starved for greed.
Rutted hill road, gravel,

affection like a trapped
paw gnawed off.

Tomorrow, I will leave you.

Dance

Linger of copper
a confessional dance
the lead of more and control

I would never. How could I? I'd lose it all.

you come when you want
match heat with heat
a hip-beat   you catch each spin off-kilter

be good
you tell me after
you've been in my mouth

Everything, the house, him, my whole everything…

dance in his living room
the bare floor exposed
dance in his kitchen

on his granite counter
once on his polished floor
on chairs   on the couch   between hours

It would be the death of a life.

taste of copper   silk threaded
tongue and cologne on my belly
so wet it could be blood

you steal the hour
if she knows she says nothing
you want me to wonder

what could be better
you wind my hair
around your hand enough to hurt

It could never be worth it. Never.

you teach me to follow by force
outside rain falls in sheets
downing rusted leaves

where they fall says nothing about them

Night, Plowing

Snow droops the hemlock boughs.
A blood patch by the house,
warm enough to melt its own impression.
Sophie brings a deer leg to the porch,
perfect in its severed self-cohesion,
and later noses through the gouged-out pelt,
gently, her mouth as soft as felt.

Her loyalty is not with us,
but with this stretch of spruce and birch,
black walnut, oak.
The cabin holds heat like a body, imperfectly.

Snow, two inches an hour—
we diagram the fire, every flicker.
Later in the plow, you say what a farce
monogamy is. Your weathered leather hat,
graying at the temples.

You think I'll disagree.
In the unbroken dark, a housecat scurries
into the bobcat's path. You build walls of snow,
send us slamming into them.

My body is the weapon we both wield.

Sophie whines into the dark.
Vanity farms, geldings, red barns
trimmed in frost, the river
and its tributaries. Your love will be
what you make it, a nest
of snakes sleeping in the walls.
Snow on hemlocks. In the morning,
barricaded roads, the frozen hearth.

Foreign Tongues

Norwegian, he says, never
gives up its grip on the tongue,
and his voice is a vice,
an accent of grief. I catch him
watching my mouth.
What does he know
of what others have lost?

Your language is like liquor,
smooth and stinging going down.
It is absorbed in the blood and gone.

He speaks in the burnt haze of sex,
his last strike before sleep.

But I remember each conjunction
that took us from here to here.
In the eye of the doomed city,
kissing a child with python arms,
the lake-black night of sirens,
codes of correspondence
deciphered by doctors.
In the skill of forgetting

who is ahead?

This need to know and be known,
the ambivalence of home—
here my own mouth is foreign.

I had forgotten
what it means to be alone
at the moment you are entered,
what it is to say what you mean.

Gift

after Derek

Give yourself tonight
to the gifts of heat and light
of desire without object
of mind without a cause
set yourself adrift
in self-forgiveness
for deeds you have not yet done
for people you have not yet hurt
perhaps not even met

tonight give yourself over to dance
give yourself music give
razor edges to balance on
tonight work with marble so your hands
and feet are the finest awls
and every finger is inlayed
with your own design
tonight put on a feast of olives
and art and unreasonable joy and know
for once the place
you've laid at the table
is for you

Piety

They will die, the ones you
love best
from murder   face-eating cancer
lungs drowned in blood   no matter

the others you save
in imagined heroisms
as though each broken fall
of someone else's father

or every wish
of health extending
into loss like a vine
bearing nothing

is a stay against it

is a comfort to anyone
but yourself
at our end
there is this sickness

we call hope

and further there is nothing
between beauty and terror
nothing half-living has

over death   and yet
the illicit thump
of every wasted heartbeat
the love of strangers

who will also die
on streets you've never seen
of wounds you couldn't heal—
their luminescent eyes in the wreckage.

Here the mountains look like mountains the ocean looks like ocean the city gleams like dragonscales
the ocean looks like ocean the city gleams like dragonscales there are trees here that grow on no other island and
fruit that tastes of salt there are trees here that grow on
no other island and fruit that tastes of salt behind the fruit market is another fruit market
where prices are never written down signs behind signs where alleys entwine with traversals

the center shifts around its other center Reclamation Streets light fixture and sequin stores
Cantopop, men cutting steel by the park in baptismal showers of sparks

Nine Dragon Island

I.

Here the mountains look like mountains
the ocean looks like ocean
the city gleams like dragonscales

there are trees here
that grow on no other island
and fruit that tastes of salt

behind the fruit market
is another fruit market
where prices are never written down

signs behind signs
where alleys entwine with traversals
the center shifts around its other center

Reclamation Street's
light fixture and sequin stores, Cantopop,
men cutting steel by the park in baptismal showers of sparks

the park is built on what used
to be city, the city
is built on what used to be a park

that park was built
on what used to be ocean
and now the ocean surrounds it

ask who built these seawalls
and bullet trains and towers
their mixes of dialects, topologies, loyalty.

II.

Today the whole of Kowloon
smells of mourning. Or do I carry
that heavy scent to every city?
The neighborhood sinks under wafts of joss.
Sacrificial ducks
tilt their dumbstruck beaks to heaven,
bowls of oranges for blessing.
Who is it who is
doing all this dying?

*

This part of the city
is made of tin but
beyond the serpentine bridge
no pedestrian can cross
are coils of neon, transmitters,
secret cameras, reinforced doors
where sunlight and gunfire
cannot penetrate the glass.

*

Under the tall shadow of Shenzhen,
the city lists to one side
with the weight of its three professions—
teaching, finance, shipping.

*

What you can buy within one block:

carambola, rambutan, durian, persimmon, pineapple, lychee, kiwi, mango, whole fruit, cut fruit, peeled fruit, dried fruit, fruit juice, fruit ice, ice cream, shaved ice, iced tea, milk tea, iced milk coffee, coconut ice cream, coconut buns, cream buns, gold and silver buns, pineapple buns, egg tart, wife cake, stinky tofu, curry chicken, chicken necks, pigs' feet, skewered fish balls, skewered pork balls, speared tofu, speared hotdogs, speared fish bits, roasted sweet potato, roasted chestnuts, soup noodles, rice noodles, fried noodles, fried pig's blood, chicken wings, baguette, banh mi, eat-in, takeout, bicycle-delivered, deliverance by woman, ladyboy, or preacher.

*

Rain, for the fifth morning in a row.
Everything green
grows readily here,
like mildew,
like ficus,
like avarice.

*

Women in heels stepping out of taxis,
businessmen betting on Louis Vuitton,
pairs of blondes in French-themed cafes,
parties in BMWs, in teahouses, in hotel suites,
babies strapped to women on buses,
on the labyrinthine pedestrian overpasses.
Skinny kids on street corners after dark.

*

City Wall Park exhibits ruins
of an ancient wall
with a fence built around it
to keep
the people out.

*

Light fixes on the water

at Victoria Bay.
The shipping magnates' tankers come
in sprays of pixelated bounty
where endless islands shimmer.
These boats bring goods,
bring oil drums, bring drugs,
bring people who bring germs
and willingness to work.

*

From a bench at Tolo Harbor
where bicyclists race by against the long blue lines
and a woman in a headscarf is mopping the promenade,
you can imagine you're seeing all the way out past Plover Cove
to the South China Sea
and somewhere beyond that is a conception of home
where people are waiting.
She looks up and out across the water,
perhaps still divining
all that is not there.

Affair

In the slow moments
after we have made love,

you peel a tangerine
and let the juice drip

onto the sheets
and your naked, smooth chest

as you hand me
the bigger half and tell me,

eat
and we'll do it again in the dark,

and leave me
with the sweet fruit slipping

down my throat, and your eyes,
shuttered like the windows,

pinning me to the bed.

Night Train

The cars haul each other
in fits and starts.
Shells of sunflowers seeds,

paper bowls of noodles.
The gift of a tangerine
its peel so thin it peels itself,

citrus oil staining
his hands. A stranger roosts
in the upper berth.

My palm reads of suffering
he says. I have never meant
a promise to be faithful.

Women offer
sweet potatoes at the station,
faces dark with coal soot.

Taste of saltpeter, bitter rind.
Station signs pass, soon
he will be gone. This mouth

of guilt would like

to know his mouth.

Only small harm will come of it.

Man in an alley off Jiangsu Lu, Shanghai

Plucking the chicken into a bucket,
he's perched on an overturned crate by the cage.
Down Anhua Lu, squawks from the survivors.

Lines of characters on a red banner
flicker in the wind and are lost. The sun
has nowhere to go but across the sky.

No scar from ruts that scored the road, before
the displaced farmers with rakes and scrapers,
buckets of asphalt. The bird is flightless,

stripped whiter than the walls have been for years.
Tonight, they'll eat the meat before it sours,
thrown to the cats that litter the alley.

Progress is ever repairing damage,
hatching more eggs to make up for the hen—
the bones and gizzard for tomorrow's soup.

Mahjong

Men don't play these wild games of mahjong.
A search for sanctuary
brings the women to the fourteenth floor
where communal breezes

come from the hall
and the open doors are draped
with torn sheets for the July
heat to escape.

Shuffled tiles whirring
like cicadas in bamboo cages,
hushed by bets.
Voices rise and recede,

the cadence of rain.
Somewhere, the children
chase each other.
The tournaments stretch from Saturday sunrise

to long past midnight.
Players rotate out
to cook distracted dinners in shifts.

Their husbands dirty

the dishes and wait
for the clatter of card table legs—
the sound of being folded up
and put out of sight.

Mangosteen

It must be the same, the peel unyielding and dark like cracked leather, the flesh musky, unpleasant, with a whiff of iodine or dry stone. The word doesn't say it. In a book of love poems someone else wrote, a drop of acid eats through the page to the past, to my temporary teacher, three years before. Jolene, she called herself then. She laughed when I tried it and the taste burned on my tongue. Mangosteen, richer than persimmon or wet-eyed longyan, rarer than *jinfoshou*, the bitter Golden Hand of the Buddha. A study of tongues, a lesson: heat, market, barter, eat. Speak, touch, taste. And that other poet, did his lover give it to him, the one he met in a bath in Beijing, fine-boned with delicate hands? Fruit and tea in the morning, after dark, after dancing. Context is all. The word arrives like the friend of a friend I'm putting up for the night. The tongue's memory fails, one of the body's countless betrayals. But I remember the taste isn't like mango, tropical but never "peach and pineapple" as Webster's has it. Jolene, whose name I never knew, she called it *shanzhu*, while other worlds went unspoken. Is this what we mean when we say the meaning of things?

Six-Foot Chopsticks

Around the corner at midnight the recyclers get to work
rooting in the heat through rotting cardboard
and unrottable bottles
their hands form conveyor belts
sending the useless to one side
and the reusable to another

this is midnight in front of the public toilet
used by neighborhood squatters just off the farm
the doors are locked each night at ten
as drunks and stray dogs lurch efficiently down the street

dinner was today's incarnation
of the daily wedding banquet or funeral feast
picking his way down the self-service buffet
Juwen says *when I was a kid an egg was extravagant*

we sit at the long table piled with dishes and talk poetry
    and politics and bad air
talk gossip and Europe and "maternity tours"
Lan says *she got so bored waiting she went to Mexico for a*
    break
and gave birth there! Think about it, what's even worse
    than a Chinese passport...

and the heat lamps slowly go out
above the salt shrimp and duck's feet and purple yam croquettes
above the fried chicken organs and pork ribs and
pastries and lychees in syrup and we are talking
about change slowly it seems we'll never leave and around us
    the tables empty
sometimes it gets so that I can't even stand the thought of meat

then fill again with women
in polyester aprons over polyester clothes
barely in the room bent over plastic bowls of rice
heaping mounds of the palest cheapest food after millet

while in the center of each table is a small metal pot
of shreds of boiled cabbage and carrot
the task of eating is finished quickly
there are the plates to collect and clean and stack for tomorrow
and they must have heard everything we say
of eggs and America and change
then it's back into the furnace of the kitchen

Fire Conforms to What It Shapes

Home again in my temporary home
I think of you again at home

with the woman who is your wife
who bore your child

to whom you say
you owe the debt

that ore owes
to its smelter

not just of gratitude
but of what can be crafted of love

and I think of you in your upstairs study
a blacksmith's shop

where the knife tries
to sharpen its edge against the stone

and I feel you for the first time
with her as man and wife

and I see this is a life
already smithed

just as your daughter
comes to your knee

to cry or whine
or finally to comfort you

with *buyao nanguo*
I was her once

in that raging forge's fire
whispering   *Dad, it's going to be ok*

and hearing his voice from the stair
no it's not

Fault Line

Torn glimpses of the city
in rough-hewn cloth
and the smell of blood, crushed

doorways open to further doorways.
Tangibles return to essence—
the calf's side

hanging in the air with flies,
a corroded coin,
wutong trees with limbs

pinned between concrete blocks.
Dust collects in pollen
and the unstoppable rain

can't sustain crops buried
under fields of tents.
Which of the world's desires

does suffering fulfill?
Poetry, you pale aper of life—
you are my comfort, not theirs.

Return

On the mud road from Yingxiu, a baby
with cheeks like two bulls-eyes of disease

clings to his mother's sleeve,
the fraught salvation

of a tent city below.
No image earns enough

for us to suffer its truth,
nothing as starved for hope

as a child weaned too soon,
his mother's body like a wound.

Hunger curls
its hand around them.

Cadavers of homes. Unknotted
neighborhood ties. Fireworks crack

like bombs in the schoolyard,
send off each buried hope in ashes

of paper money and women
gripping photographs,

fathers folded away from themselves.
The mind's aperture opens

to arms like cut cornstalks
reaching through dust.

Yet, yet...press an ear to these walls—
lost whispers of drinking songs,

the clack of mahjong tiles,
the unearthed skeleton of tomorrow.

Beggars Outside the Chengdu Train Station at Noon

The boy's swelled belly and burnt cheeks
say hunger. *Auntie*, he calls me

while the old woman watches,
a hand outstretched.

His mother is elsewhere
or dead. I give bread, I give

the bananas I've bought for the train.
The man with stumps for legs

wheels himself past on a cart
of cracked boards nailed flat—

"Can't you tell he isn't hers? Just take him,
give him the good American life."

She offers him up, willing
to bargain. But what is *good*, and who

thinks such leaden
ontological thoughts?

The need for relief
from guilt runs deep—

no merit will come from this charity,
though even the emperor thinks it will.

The boy's eyes blink pigeon-red,
too empty even to scavenge for love.

Hope

the way the dark-bellied
dew lover clings
to an apricot stem

and in the sudden gale
from some careless
human mouth

hunkers down flat
tucks in its fragile wings
and holds on

In Praise of Dumplings

Chopping Chinese leeks,
my eyes, back-sighted, blur.
The cold cut of your voice

saying the dice should be finer
or the flavors won't marry.
You always did

wield the knife better.
You formed the dough
as your grandmother did

in her outdoor kitchen,
the flies like children
buzzing at her elbows,

the *dofu* fermenting in a pail,
the bamboo cut, coming up again.
You rolled, I folded,

our cross-purposes
for once synchronized.
In the pungency of white pepper,

the sting of ginger and scallion,
I salt and boil the water,
drop dumplings into the sea.

You'd scoop each out with a spoon
translucent, vulnerable
as shelled oysters,

your hands unflinching in the steam.
I remember those fingers
on my instep. *Little Bodhisattva feet,*

but all these calluses!
You thought I was careless,
but I cared beyond reason,

stopped to question devotion
too late to salvage a shared life.
Now I make

the dumplings alone,
as I like them,
quiet in this quiet house.

On the Second Day of Her Trip to Beijing, My Mother Loses a Tooth

Once that soft exposed socket
and swallowed blood were exciting
the wound would heal
barely a wound at all

and the lack of something that was
would be replaced with
greater and sharper things

now what is gone
is gone
you accept it with admirable calm

(still at dinner with the others
you hide your mouth when you laugh)

and for all this parallel guilt
there is nothing I can bring back to you
nothing to be said now or forgiven

all I can offer is ibuprofen and water
one pink peach in perfect blush
that you grasp in your hand tight as a trap

you ask me to wait so I wait

watching you in your nightgown
hair down and silver
slowly readying yourself
for whatever is next

Discipline

Banished
to Sichuan's dark peaks beyond
the court's reach,

he gestures
for a sheaf of rice paper,
brush and ink,

an inkwell of stone
broken open, hollowed smooth
where the ink pools.

He dips the brush,
draws the end on the stone's
rim for a tip.

The body becomes
an eggshell of spine, inside
a mind quivers

which is the same
mind proving its nature
in characters.

The hand stills,
rice paper dries puckered in silence.
He suddenly feels the cold.

Then, Something

These narrowed streets I once called home
are home to others now. Their words begin

to fail me. I cannot bring a self to mind.
In piles of bricks crushed by feet

a dog noses for trash, a beggar
picks his way across the filthy puddles.

Easy to cling to these desires,
to covet their fruits

like the parrot who strains in silence
against his perch-chained claw. The sun

savors its strength, a humid breeze
teases the heat through peach trees,

flinging blessings everywhere.